Mozart for a Mother's Soul

By Teresa B. Kindred

Illustrated by Beth O'Bryant

Design by Lesley Ehlers

Peter Pauper Press, Inc.
White Plains, New York

For Mama with love

The text of this title originally appeared in a
Peter Pauper Press Keepsake entitled A Mother's
Prayer, *published in 1995.*

The Station, on page 7, *is excerpted from* A Penny's
Worth of Minced Ham, *copyright © 1986 by*
Southern Illinois University Press, Carbondale, IL
62902-3697. All rights reserved.
Reprinted by permission.

Text copyright © 1995, 1996
Peter Pauper Press, Inc.
202 Mamaroneck Avenue
White Plains, NY 10601
Illustrations copyright © 2000
Beth O'Bryant
All rights reserved
ISBN 0-88088-413-4
Printed in China
7   0   5   4

Visit us at www.peterpauper.com

Table of Contents

A Mother's Prayer ❦ *6*

Summer ❦ *10*

Mama's Love ❦ *14*

Rules for Mothers ❦ *19*

A Role Model ❦ *26*

Cabin Fever ❦ *28*

The Things They Say ❦ *33*

My Middle Child ❦ *38*

A Double Helping of Love ❦ *41*

Sticky Fingers on the Window ❦ *46*

Cousins ❦ *49*

Making Music My Way ❦ *53*

Dear Lord,

Help me keep my priorities straight. Remind me that spending time with my children is more important than anything else I can do. Let me sit down and read books to them without seeing the dust and dirt in the corners of my house. Help me realize that the day is coming soon when my children won't all be under one roof. Then I will long for the days when I knew where they were, what they were doing, and the precious moments we all shared together.

Amen

A Mother's Prayer

From the time I found out I was expecting my first child I began to keep a journal. I wanted my child to know that from the very first moment he was loved. Since that first journal I have filled three books and had four more children.

From time to time I go back and read the pages that chronicle my life. Often I find myself laughing at something that at the time didn't seem like a laughing matter. Like the time I came home from church and took the roast, potatoes, and carrots out of the oven and promptly dumped them on the floor.

Sometimes when I read my journal I cry. I am reminded of how very close we came to losing our daughter to meningitis when she was only seven months old. Or how painful it was to watch my mother become ill with the cancer that eventually took her life.

Tucked between two pages of my journal is a single page torn out of a magazine years ago. It was condensed from a book called *The Station*, by Robert J. Hastings, and it compares life to being on a train.

Looking out the windows and watching life go by we dream of our destination, says Hastings. "At a certain hour and on a given day, our train will finally pull into the station . . . And once that day comes, so many wonderful dreams will come true. . . . 'Yes, when we reach the station, that will be it!' we promise ourselves. 'When we're eighteen . . . win that promotion . . . buy that 450 SL Mercedes Benz . . . have a nest egg for retirement.' From that day on we will all live happily ever after. Sooner or later, however, we must realize that there is no station in this life, no one earthly place to arrive at once and for all. The journey is the joy. The station is an illusion—it constantly outdistances us."

If we wait for the perfect moment, the perfect life, we are bound to be disappointed. Nothing on earth is perfect. That doesn't mean we can't find happiness in this life. It just means we won't find perfection.

When I look at my journal I see some good days and some bad days. Not perfection. One day when I have completed my trip and my children read my journals, I hope they realize that my life was made sweeter because of them. They were the roses that I stopped to smell along the way. They were the joy that made my journey worthwhile.

∽*T.B.K.*

Summer

*S*omeone asked me what my favorite season was. Without a moment's hesitation I answered "summer." Don't get me wrong. I like the freshness of spring, the glamour of fall, and I like the feeling of being closed in with my family during a winter snow storm, at least for a day or two. But nothing compares to summer.

What do I like best about it? The sights, sounds, and smells that make it so real you can taste it. If summer were an ice cream flavor I'm sure I could eat a gallon a day.

I love the feel of grass beneath my bare feet. Fireflies twinkling in the darkness. Roasting hot dogs and marshmallows on coat hangers over an open fire. Family volleyball, with lots of yelling and laughter. The soft patter of rain drops as they hit the tree leaves in the forest. The fresh smell of the air after a gentle summer shower. My children's laughter as it drifts across the back yard and through my open kitchen window. The feeling (even if it's only short-lived) that summer will last forever.

It doesn't. Reality comes in the form of the first "Back to School" catalog. Flashy ads with happy kids dressed in new school clothes remind me that my favorite season is about to disappear.

While my children are getting excited over new school clothes, I'm dreading getting up at 6:00 a.m. While they are looking forward to seeing their friends again, I'm wondering how I'll ever get them out of bed, dressed, and to school on time.

Maybe it's not the sights, smells, and sounds of summer that cause me to love it after all. Maybe it's the feeling of not being rushed. Once school starts I'm back on the merry-go-round of ball games, club meetings, PTA, etc. In the summer there's a more relaxed feeling of what I don't get done today I *can* do tomorrow.

It's not often that I wish I could turn back the clock one

hundred years. Mainly because I'm not sure I could exist without running water and electricity. Even so, somewhere there is a part of me that yearns for a simpler life.

I picture a white farm house with a big front porch and a wooden swing. A place where I sit and watch the fireflies at dusk and smell the freshly-cut hay. A place where all I have to do is sit and watch my children grow. A place where summer lasts forever.

Mama's Love

Mother's Day has been difficult for me since Mama died. I am not reminded of the joys of being a mother when the Hallmark commercials come on television this time of year, but rather the sadness I feel from not having my mother with me.

What I miss the most is sharing my children with her. I get a twinge of sadness because I was never able financially to give her a tiny fraction of what she gave to me. My Mother's Day gifts to her were usually inexpensive and simple. I thought about this yesterday when my seven-year-old thanked me for his birthday presents. "Mom," he said, "do you know which gift I liked the best?"

I imagined it would be the super soaker water gun. Guaranteed to shoot up to fifty feet. I know it shoots at least that far, because he managed to douse his sister, the dog, and me, while we were running from him. I was wrong. It wasn't the water gun.

"It's the love you gave me Mom," he stated, then ran off to play.

I stood with my mouth open and the tears streaming down my face, feeling overwhelmed with how wonderful motherhood can be. I longed to pick up the phone and call the person who was my mother and my best friend. I wanted to tell her that the love she gave to me lives on in my children. Then I realize that my love, and the love of her grandchildren, were the only gifts she wanted.

Mama's love for me lives on in other ways too. When the flowers bloom in our yard the perennials she planted only months before she died reappear. She knew she would never live to see them bloom again. She planted flowers for others to enjoy.

Her love comes to me from her former elementary school students. For seventeen years she touched the lives of young children. They remember her and come to tell me what a positive influence she was in their lives.

One of my clearest memories of Mama occurred the night the doctor came to her room and told us she had cancer. First we prayed. She looked at me, held my hand and said softly, "I wanted to buy Rachel's first prom dress."

My daughter Rachel was six years old at the time. It wasn't really the dress that was important to her. It was the fact she wouldn't be there to watch her granddaughter grow up.

Each Mother's Day I have bittersweet memories. I rejoice in the knowledge that I had a mother who loved me and taught me right from wrong. And I cry because I miss her friendship, her strength, her humor, and her love of my children.

I made a promise to myself the day she died. When my daughter is a teenager I will take her shopping for a prom dress. I will pay for the dress with Mama's money, and I will tell Rachel that the dress is a gift from her grandmother. Then I will tell her love never

dies. It keeps growing from one generation to the next.

I have a feeling that Mama will be watching on that day and she'll smile.

Rules for Mothers

A few weeks ago I went to our state's Beta Convention as one of the high school's Beta Club sponsors. Except for not getting much sleep, it was a good trip. I enjoy being around teenagers, but I confess that I came home feeling envious of them. No, I don't want to be sixteen again. I lived through that once. I am envious of the time they have to share with their friends. At this stage in my life even a phone conversation with a friend is impossible unless it is between the hours of 12:00 midnight and 6:00 a.m. Since I am comatose after 10 p.m., that doesn't work either. When I was sixteen I could stay up that late without any problem. Now if I'm up at those hours it's because one of the kids is throwing up.

I miss the camaraderie of friendship. It's wonderful to have someone listen to your troubles and sympathize. The only time I get sympathy from my children is if a program I want to watch on television is pre-empted by the President giving a press conference. In their minds that's a tragedy.

There are a few simple rules I've discovered to help me survive this period in my life.

1. Mothers never get sick. Mothers don't have the time.

2. Mothers never have anything important to do. I don't care if you're the best paid lawyer in the largest law firm in America and you're about to try a case that has been on every major network for ten weeks, it's not important. If little Johnny has a ball game and he needs you to take him there, skip the trial.
(See rule number 5)

3. Mothers are never allowed to complain. Even if you left the trial and took him to the ball game, don't tell him how much you sacrificed or how much he should appreciate you. They don't care.

Compare this to the story your parents told you when you were small. You know, the one about walking through ten feet of snow barefoot to get to school. Aha, now you understand.

4. Supper should always be ready when the kids are ready to eat. Be prepared to serve every child individually because they are never hungry at the same time. Don't serve vegetables. Junk food is preferred. I once served five kinds of vegetables straight from the garden (not my garden, but somebody's garden). My son turned up his nose and said, "How disgusting! Healthy stuff! Not even any french fries!"

5. The car should always have plenty of gas in it and you should be ready to act as chauffeur at a moment's notice. This can be complicated when you have one car and five children who need to be in different places at the same time. Leave an hour before they need to be at their destination and don't slow down except for stop

signs. You should make it okay.

6. Clothes should be clean, neatly pressed and put where the kids can find them. The best location is the floor since that is where they usually leave them.

7. Moms are not allowed in the bathroom unless no one else has to go. A solution for this problem is to add another bathroom to your house, which will cost you a small fortune. Or you can buy a port-a-potty. They aren't very attractive but they're a lot cheaper.

Some day the kids will be grown, and there will be time for friendship again. Until then please don't call my house unless it's between midnight and 6 a.m.

Dear Lord,

I pray for the children of the world who
face seemingly insurmountable obstacles.
Be with them and give them the courage
and strength that they need to survive.
Teach them Your ways and shower them
with love. No matter what color their skin,
what language they speak, what religion
they adhere to, whether they are rich or
poor, they are *all* Your children.

∽ *Amen*

Beth O'Bryant

A Role Model

Every young girl has someone she looks up to, someone she wants to grow up to be like. For me it was Kate. Maybe it was because she was a teenager when I was barely ten. The sound of the word "teenager" seemed exciting to me. She was everything I thought was cool. She listened to Elvis. She was a cheerleader, and her boyfriend was *awfully* cute.

Another reason I admired her was because she took the time to listen to me. Cousin Martha and I would follow her around (we even spied on her a couple of times). I'm sure we were a nuisance, but she never acted as if we were.

When Kate went away to college she invited us to visit. Martha and I thought we were so grown up to be on a college campus. Even after she married she was brave enough to invite the two of us to come for a week. We went swimming in the apartment complex pool, and hung out in her apartment while she went to work. Freedom, how we loved it.

I don't see her often now, but I think about her a lot. I wonder if she knows she did a good job as a role model.

I look at my own daughter who is now nine, and wonder who she will look up to. I hope it's someone who will take the time to be a friend to her. Someone like Kate.

Cabin Fever

It snowed six inches last Monday and the temperature has hovered around zero for days.

It's been a long week. The first few days we were snowed in were fun. I cleaned out closets, slept late, and actually managed to stay awake at night long enough to watch the news. After day three, things began to get a little hairy. My nerves became jangled and my temper short. The kids were pretty good considering they hadn't been out of the house except to build a snowman and throw a few snowballs. It wasn't the kids. It was me. I had a full-blown case of "cabin fever."

Finally the roads were clear enough to make it to Wal-Mart. It's amazing what a little shopping, eating out, and a change of scenery can do for my personality. I felt almost human again.

Sometimes I get frustrated by people who look at me and shake their heads in awe and say, "You have five children. How do you manage?" As if I knew all the secrets to being a perfect mother. Believe me I don't. Having five children doesn't make me Super Mom. Like everybody else, I cope. I do the best I can, and some days my best isn't good enough.

Weeks like this past one are trying. No matter how many times I vow I won't lose my patience, I do. I pray for patience every night. Besides Hershey's chocolate kisses with almonds and Mars bars it's the one thing I can't have enough of.

I do have some advantages when it comes to being a mother of five. I have a wonderful husband who helps (and many other family members who pitch in). I had a mother who was a good role model, and I believe God is there for me and is helping me raise my little ones. Not every one is lucky enough to have the first two advantages, but everyone can have the last one.

I guess I wasn't a total failure this week. The kids have enjoyed the snow, staying up late, and not going to school. Friday our oldest son looked up from his sixth pizza of the week and sighed, "Gee Mom, this has been the best week of my life."

I guess "cabin fever" is an adult's disease.

The Things They Say

One of the hardest things about being a mother is knowing when to laugh at something your children say and when not to. If I'm not careful I forget that often the funny things they say are very serious matters for them. Often it's Justin who comes up with some off-the-wall comment that causes me to want to smile.

"Mom," Justin said thoughtfully, "I'm going with somebody."

I stopped what I was doing and turned to him. I knew what "going with somebody" meant. I wasn't sure he did.

"Is that okay?" he asked hesitantly.

Silently I wondered how many years it would be before he stopped asking me if it was okay to go with someone.

"Justin, just what do you think going with someone means?" I asked.

"It means chasing them at the playground during P.E." he answered. "Then when I'm twelve I get to kiss her."

I doubt if he'll be chasing the same girl when he's twelve, but chasing them at the playground is okay with me.

Another night this week Justin came running in from playing and his face was streaked with dirt and grime. "Justin, you have to have a bath," I said.

"Why?" he questioned.

"Because you are dirty and you stink," I answered.

"But Mom," he moaned, "Why do I have to have a bath just because I stink?"

After arguing the issue for several minutes he got a pencil and paper and wrote me a note which he posted on the refrigerator. It read, "Dear Mom and Dad. Good By I love you Justin."

"Does this mean you are leaving home?" I asked him.

"Yes it does," he said firmly. "Right after I take my bath."

Justin didn't run away. He couldn't since he's not allowed to go past the two big maple trees at the end of our drive. If he had tried to leave I wouldn't have let him. Some day the time will come for him to venture out into the world, but not yet. I want to keep him all to myself just a little longer. I like the way he makes me want to smile.

Dear Lord,

Thank you for all the seasons. Walk with me through the spring and summer of my life and be with me during fall and winter. When I complain or grow weary with winter gently remind me that, "To every thing there is a season, and a time to every purpose under the heaven." *(Ecclesiastes 3:1)* (KJV)

Amen

My Middle Child

There have been many studies about the birth order of children affecting their personalities. Even if I hadn't read some of these studies, I could still tell you that the middle child generally gets the least amount of attention. My husband and I make a conscious effort to make our third child, Justin, feel special. It's not hard to do because he *is* special.

When people look at our family they see Nick as the oldest, Rachel as the only girl, and Russell and Grant as "the twins." They don't always see Justin for what he is: a child who marches to the beat of a different drummer. Unlike his siblings, who love to squabble, Justin is the peacemaker. He wants everyone to be happy. Especially his mom. He often neglects his own wishes to make things go smoother. If the other kids want pepperoni pizza and he wants sausage, he'll eat pepperoni to keep everyone happy.

He has a unique perspective of the world. One day I was expecting company and the house was a mess. "Justin," I asked, "what kind of shape is the basement in?" He looked at me seriously and replied, "Last time I looked, Mom, it was a rectangle."

When he was three he had all kinds of questions about God and Heaven. He told me that God had a ladder that He climbed to get up to Heaven. He was also sure God had toys in Heaven. After all, it wouldn't be Heaven without toys.

One morning after about ten trips up and down the stairs to fetch jeans for one child, shoes for another, a hair brush for still another, I yelled out in frustration, "I quit!" Justin looked at me with his big blue eyes and in a tiny voice that broke my heart said, "You mean you want to quit being my mom?"

No, Justin, I will never stop being your mom. I will never stop loving you. My love is unconditional. It will last longer than I can live because it is forever.

A Double Helping of Love

When Bill and I found out we were expecting twins, we were excited, and apprehensive. One more baby seemed like a good idea. Two more seemed overwhelming. Something our oldest son said changed my outlook. One night we were talking and Nick said, "You know Mom, God must think we're mighty special to send us two babies at once." After that I looked at things in a different light.

There is something *special* about twins. Instead of one cute, cuddly infant there are two. Two sets of night feedings, first words, first steps, dirty diapers, and when they cry, it's in stereo.

Before Russell and Grant were born, I vowed not to dress them alike and I haven't, very often. People are fascinated by twins. They want to talk about them, comment on them, tell me about someone they know who has twins. Usually the stories involve a sense of wonder because of the closeness twins exhibit, in between bouts of biting and hitting.

I know that when most people look at Russell and Grant they see twins. When I look at them I see two little boys who just happen to be the same age. I don't see a good twin, and a bad twin, or any other significant differences. Just two little boys who have made my life more wonderful every day of their existence.

One of the best feelings in the world is the softness of a baby's hair as you rub your face against it. When Russell and Grant were small their hair reached a certain stage in length where it stood straight up all over their heads. Heaven on earth for me was rubbing my nose in that soft hair. I was almost sorry when it grew long enough to lie down. I was really sorry when it grew long enough to be cut. If our beautician were not such a gracious lady she probably would tell us to take our business elsewhere. If you

raise your windows on the days the twins get hair cuts I'm sure you can hear them screaming, no matter where you are.

From the moment they were born and I counted all twenty fingers and twenty toes, I have never gotten over how wonderful it is to have twins. At night when I read them their bedtime story, and they put their little hands together and say their "Now I lay me down to sleep" prayer, I pray too. I look at their two little bowed heads, and I thank God for my littlest angels.

Yes, my life is complicated. It means I have to re-evaluate my priorities daily. If something isn't *really* important, it doesn't get done. One of the first things to go was baking. I never liked it anyway, so it was no great sacrifice. I didn't realize just how much my cooking had slipped until one day this week my daughter baked a cake. Russell and Grant just couldn't wait to eat it so I gave them each a big slice and they promptly broke out into strains of "Happy Birthday." Poor little fellows. They think cake is only for birthdays.

Sometimes Russell and Grant play a game where they argue with one another. One will say, "My Mommy," and the other will say, "No. My Mommy," and they'll go on and on until they get tired of it. There are some days when I feel like I'm "Mommy" to the whole world. But even on those days I wouldn't trade being their "Mommy" for anything in the world.

Sticky Fingers on the Window

*Twenty years ago I couldn't stand country music. When I was a teenager it just wasn't "cool." I can't bear to listen to that stuff teenagers listen to now. I refuse to call it music. Most of the time I listen to a radio station that plays "oldies," which really makes me feel ancient since it's mostly music from my adolescent years. When I get tired of "oldies" I listen to country. At least you can understand the words to most of the songs.

One of the songs I like the most describes the hands of a father. I don't remember the words exactly but it says something about a father using his hands to correct his child with kindness and love. Our hands say a lot about us. When I hear this song I think about my own father's hands. His weathered, calloused hands clearly show the hard labor he's been accustomed to every day of his life. I think of his hands as being strong, and protecting. When I picture them holding my children I see them as being gentle, almost tender.

My brother Robert told me once that Mama used to sit in church and hold his hand. Every so often she would whisper and tell him how beautiful his hands were. He always replied, "No, they're not, Mom." "Oh yes, they are," she'd argue. "The things they can do are beautiful."

Hands are beautiful. When they're helping hands or when they're healing hands, giving the touch of comfort to someone who needs an encouraging touch. Sometimes they're beautiful just because they're there. There's nothing more comforting than the feel of someone's hand in yours as you walk through this life.

And then there are the most beautiful hands of all. The ones that leave sticky finger prints on the windows. The ones that smear peanut butter and jelly on your new blouse. The ones that hold on to your leg when you're trying to get off to work in the morning.

The ones that fit together and point upward when they whisper their "Now I lay me down to sleep" prayers. The ones that go around your neck and squeeze tightly while they whisper the words that make every moment of motherhood worthwhile: "I love you Mom."

Cousins

Summer vacation has officially arrived. The children have been out of school one week, and already I'm hearing, "What can we do? I'm bored."

It sounds familiar. I said the same thing myself to my mother not so many years ago. It seems like only yesterday that summer vacation stretched before me beckoning with days and days of endless possibilities.

As a child summer meant chasing fireflies at night, and running barefoot. It meant eating watermelon and seeing who could spit the seeds the farthest, making mud pies and decorating them with grass and rocks. Summer was a time for playing tag and Red Rover at my grandfather's house. And the very best part of all, the climax to the whole summer, was when my cousins from Florida came up to visit.

My cousin Martha and I are the same age. We spent countless hours in each other's company. We were the oldest grandchildren, and the only girls, so we bossed the younger boy cousins unmercifully. We played "Let's Pretend" behind some bushes in my grandfather's yard where we dined regally on cookies and milk. We spent warm summer nights in the upstairs bedroom gossiping and giggling with the fan in the window whirring monotonously for background music. In the early morning the sound of the rooster crowing awakened us from girlish dreams. We shared the pains of growing up, of being together a few weeks, then separated for months, when she and her family went back to Florida.

For several years during our late teens we grew apart. Our lives took different paths. But that common bond of childhood, and family, remained strong. We were in each other's weddings, had children about the same time, and when my greatest sorrow came

and Mama died, Martha was there to hold my hand. After the funeral she spent the night with me and we read letters Mama had written to me while I was away at college. We laughed and cried and grieved as only two people who have shared a lifetime of memories together can. When Martha comes to visit now she brings her three children and stays at my house instead of my grandfather's. I have five children so we spend a lot of time preparing peanut butter and jelly sandwiches, and picking up paper plates and dirty clothes. But we still manage to find time to go for walks, and talk, and share dreams together.

When my children come running to me and tell me they're bored I try to be patient. Because years from now when they look back on their childhood memories of summer I have a feeling they won't remember being bored. They'll remember chasing fireflies at night, eating watermelon and spitting the seeds, and especially those few weeks when their cousins came to visit.

Making Music My Way

✦

I will never be a painter. I'm not even an art connoisseur. I will never have a Picasso, or Rembrandt, hanging in my living room. I do have a strong feeling about what I like, and I have a deep admiration for the talent it takes to create a work of art.

I will never be a singer. When I was little and someone would ask me what I wanted to be when I grew up, I would answer "a singer." It didn't take long for reality to take care of that ambition. I can listen to those who can sing, and appreciate their talent. I think Barbra Streisand is wonderful. The power in her voice amazes me. She can make me feel the music in my heart.

I can't paint. I can't sing, and I certainly can't dance. We have to find a way to make our own music, to sing our own song. I make my music on a keyboard, not a piano or organ, but a computer keyboard. For me there are very few things in life that equal the high I get when someone says, "You know, I really enjoyed reading something you wrote. It made me feel . . ." For a writer there is no greater reward than to make someone feel.

As I watch my children grow and search for their identity, I can't help but wonder how they will make their music. Will they sing or dance, or maybe be the next Picasso?

It doesn't matter. What matters is that when they find their talent they use it. No one succeeds without two things—belief in oneself and persistence. Calvin Coolidge probably said it best. "Nothing in the world can take the place of persistence. Talent will not; nothing is more common than unsuccessful men of talent. Genius will not; unrewarded genius is almost a proverb. Education will not; the world is full of educated derelicts. Persistence and determination alone are omnipotent."

There are many things I want my children to have. Faith, obedience, love for their fellow man, and determination. The world is full of people who will discourage you and tell you something is impossible. I want my children to be able to look back at the doubters and say, "I can."

Nothing can stop them from making their music. Whatever song they may sing.

Dear Lord,

Of all the tasks I will undertake in my lifetime, there is none more important to me than being a good mother. Please guide me every step of the way. Remind me that my every word and deed is being watched by my children. My life must be a pattern for them to follow. No matter what I achieve in my life it will not matter if I fail as a mother. Please help me get it right.

∽ *Amen*

Mozart for a Mother's Soul

1. Eine Kleine Nachtmusik—Allegro   5:46
2. Eine Kleine Nachtmusik—Romanze: Andante   5:25
3. Eine Kleine Nachtmusik—Rondo   4:08
   Erich Leinsdorf/Boston Symphony
4. Violin Concerto No. 5, 3rd Movement: Rondeau   8:56
   Vladimir Spivakov
5. Piano Sonata in C, K. 545, 1st Movement   3:05
   Alicia de Larrocha
6. Symphony No. 40—Allegro molto   5:44
   Jean Francois Paillard/English Chamber Orchestra
7. Clarinet Concerto in A, K. 622—Adagio   8:36
   Richard Stoltzman, clarinet; Alexander Schneider/
   English Chamber Orchestra
8. Violin Concerto No. 3—Adagio   7:44
   Gidon Kremer, violin/conductor/Vienna Symphony
9. The Marriage of Figaro: Overture   4:12
   Bavarian Radio Symphony Orchestra

I hope this book
brings you peace & serenity.
You are loved.

Judy

To
Julia
From
Judy